IMAGES
of America

TROY

AERIAL VIEW OF TROY (TOP) SHOWING MOUNT IDA TO THE RIGHT. Troy was a major industrial city up until the 1950s, as shown here. The historic Hudson River forms the western border of the city. The Congress Street bridge connected Watervliet (lower center) to Troy, while the Green Island bridge connected the Village of Green Island, crossing Center Island (middle left).

PRE-CHRISTMAS SHOPPING DAYS ON THIRD STREET LOOKING NORTH IN THE LATE 1960S. The buildings on the right are now the Atrium. Downtown Troy was a busy place before urban renewal of the late 1960s and 1970s.

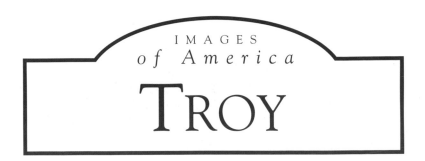

IMAGES
of America

TROY

Don Rittner

ARCADIA

First printed 1998.

Published by Arcadia Publishing,
an imprint of Tempus Publishing, Inc.
2 Cumberland Street
Charleston, SC 29401

Printed in Great Britain.

Library of Congress Catalog Card Number: 98-88053

For all general information contact Arcadia Publishing at:
Telephone 843-853-2070
Fax 843-853-0044
E-Mail sales@arcadiapublishing.com

For customer service and orders:
Toll-Free 1-888-313-2665

Visit us on the internet at http://www.arcadiaimages.com

*To the people of Troy who made their history,
and to the Rensselaer County Historical Society for preserving it!*

THE CREW ABOARD THE NORTHERN CIVIL WAR SHIP, MONITOR. It defeated *Merrimack* at the famous sea battle of Hampton Roads in 1862. The plates for this ship were made at the Albany Iron Works in Troy. John Griswold, John F. Winslow, and Capt. John Ericsson, the designer of *Monitor*, are given credit on a plaque at Monument Square. Both the Albany Iron Works and Rensselaer Iron Works contributed to the effort.

CONTENTS

Introduction   7

1.   Cityscapes, Landmarks, and Views of Troy   9

2.   Troy's Industries and Merchants   41

3.   Transportation and Movement   61

4.   Institutions:
     Charitable, Educational, Religious, and Civic   83

5.   People and Events   97

6.   Recreation and Leisure   111

7.   Disasters   121

MAP OF DOWNTOWN TROY, 1858. This is Troy shortly before the great fire of 1862, which burned most of the downtown business district.

INTRODUCTION

"The Present is specious, the Future is unknown. The Past is all we have."
—Anonymous

Welcome to the city of Troy, New York, located about 150 miles up the Hudson River from New York City. Troy has been called "The Collar City," "Home of Uncle Sam," and "The Birthplace of the American Industrial Revolution." All of these titles have merit. Troy has a rich industrial history that has its roots in the entrepreneurial spirit of the post-Revolutionary War period of the United States.

This book is not a narrative history of the city of Troy. There have been several written histories that have done justice to Troy's early years, in particular by authors Arthur Weise, Rutherford Hayner, Nathaniel Sylvester, and George Baker Anderson. This is a picture book, with more than two hundred historical photographs of Troy's cityscape, landmarks, people, and events. If it is true that a picture is worth a thousand words, then the book does tell quite a story.

I have arranged the photographs so that they are geographically related, therefore, you can use the book as a walking historical field trip. This allows you to see first hand the changing face of Troy over time. Most of the book focuses on downtown Troy. A few sites need to be visited by car or by exploring off road. The majority of the photographs cover the last half of the 19th century and first quarter of the 20th century when Troy was at its heyday as an industrial giant.

Troy has a great history. In two hundred years, Troy has undergone a transformation. Originally farmland at the end of the Revolutionary War, to an industrial center by the time of the Civil War, to an economically-deprived city two decades after the close of World War II. The city is working hard to recover from the effects of urban renewal during the 1960s and 1970s, which decimated much of the downtown business district. But, like the ancient city it was named for—itself reborn at least nine times—Troy, New York is working hard to rebuild itself as a center for education and high technology thanks to Rensselaer Polytechnic Institute (RPI), one of the great engineering schools in the country, which began in Troy in 1824. The entrepreneurial spirit has never left Troy. Today, thousands of people flock to Troy for celebrations like the summer River Fest or fall Victorian Stroll. Troy has maintained its beautiful riverfront and several economic development proposals are in the works to bring back its beautiful downtown.

Troy was incorporated as a village in 1798 with a handful of people living within its borders. By 1816, the year Troy became a city, its population was over four thousand. Before the 19th century was out, more than 70,000 people lived and worked in the city. When historians discuss Troy they point to its diversity of architecture (almost every style can be found here), to the 19th-century advances in iron and steel technology (Burden Iron Works, the Bessemer Steel process), to the development of the collar, cuff, and shirt industry (first detachable collars, Cluett, Peabody, & Co.), to the contributions to peace (development of the ironclad *Monitor*, military leaders like John E. Wool and Joseph B. Carr), and even to national symbols like "Uncle Sam" Wilson, who packed beef for the troops during the War of 1812. While those are simple highlights, there are hundreds of additional examples of the ingenuity and resourcefulness of the citizens of Troy that made this city famous worldwide for so many years. The photographs in this book are a mere sample of those contributions.

Today, Troy includes the village of Lansingburgh. Lansingburgh, or "New City" as it was called (in contrast to "Old City," Albany, just south of it), has the distinction of being the first settlement on the eastern banks of the Hudson River in Rensselaer County. In fact, Lansingburgh was a thriving mercantile village when the area of Troy was still the farmland of three brothers of Dutch descent: Matthias, Jacob I., and Jacob D. Van der Heyden. The village was annexed to the city of Troy in 1900. Because Lansingburgh has its own rich history, it will be the subject of its own pictorial history.

Most of the photographs in this book are from the rich archives of the Rensselaer County Historical Society. Those that are not are from the Morris Gerber Collection, or my own, including those on pages 38 (top), 43 (both), 54 (both), 55 (top), 57 (bottom), 60 (bottom), and 88 (bottom). The book has been arranged into seven categories that include landscapes, landmarks, views, industries and merchants, transportation, institutions (educational, religious, and civic), people and events, recreation, and disasters. I have tried to select examples that show an active city economically and socially. I have tried to find the best possible representations of each with small explanations, but any errors are my own. The quality of the original photographs (and photographers) varies. Where exact dates are known, they are included.

It is my hope that this book will make you look at Troy in a different light and develop a better understanding and appreciation for the contributions Troy has made to a developing nation. It is also hoped that you will develop a deep commitment to preserve what is left of this rich history. What makes any community different from the rest is the synergism created by its people and the environment they create. No two cities look alike. No two cities have the same history. Troy is unique in that it still has so much of its historic fabric intact. Let us insure that future generations will be able to enjoy it. Support the Rensselaer County Historical Society and other organizations that have dedicated themselves to preserving this rich heritage on the Hudson.

To learn more about the excellent collections and work of the Rensselaer County Historical Society, contact them at 57 Second Street, Troy, New York, 12180.

If you have any historic photographs or memorabilia of Troy that you would like to share, or if you would like to discuss this book, please contact me via email at DRITTNER@aol.com or by mail at P.O. Box 50216, Albany, New York, 12205.

Special thanks are extended to all of the wonderful staff at the Rensselaer County Historical Society in Troy, New York, for their patience, guidance, and help in preparing this book. All but a few of the photographs in this book are from their superb collection. I want to especially thank Curator Stacy Pomeroy Draper and Registrar Kathy Sheehan for their personal attention and help in making sure errors are few.

Don Rittner
August 1998

One

CITYSCAPES, LANDMARKS, AND VIEWS OF TROY

FULTON MARKET BUILDING, INTERSECTION OF FULTON STREET (ELBOW STREET UNTIL 1847) AND RIVER STREET LOOKING SOUTHWEST. Built in 1840, by the city, it was one of three public markets throughout Troy. It was first occupied in 1841 on the first floor by butchers and marketers. The upper floors were used as a lecture hall, for concerts, and for theater. The site was sold to William H. Frear on August 4, 1879. Previous to the erection of the market building it was a public shipyard.

MARKET BLOCK LOOKING SOUTH UP RIVER STREET. The public market is on the right in disrepair. Harmony Hall is on the left, built in 1850 by Nathan Dauchy. Notice the trolley and wagon competing for the same space.

MARKET BLOCK LOOKING NORTH UP RIVER STREET, INTERSECTION OF FULTON (ELBOW) STREET ON THE RIGHT. The Boardman building is at right in this image, *c.* 1882. In 1847 the Troy, or Peale's, Museum opened here on August 23, 1847. The first U.S. presentation of Uncle Tom's Cabin was performed here in 1852. All of the buildings viewed here are now gone, victims of urban renewal in the 1960s and 1970s. M. Timpane (banner seen on building) was a watchmaker and jeweler.

FULTON MARKET FROM FULTON (ELBOW) STREET LOOKING WEST, C. 1887–1903. Frear's Cash Bazaar is to the left and the Boardman building is to the right. Notice the photographer getting ready to shoot.

NATIONAL STATE BANK. It replaced the Fulton Market building in 1904. State Bank of Troy was the 11th bank started in the city, in 1852. Originally located on the southeast corner of First and State Streets, it became the National State Bank in 1865. Various types of companies have used the building over the years.

AMERICAN HOTEL OR HOUSE, BUILT IN 1835, SOUTHEAST CORNER OF FULTON AND THIRD STREETS. It was called the Frear House until William H. Frear tore it down to build the present Frear's Cash Bazaar building in 1897. As early as 1798, Mason's Arms, an inn owned by Joseph Munn, occupied the site. This photograph was taken *c.* 1897.

THIRD STREET LOOKING NORTHWEST. American Hotel is in the distance. On the right is the Griswold Opera House, named for John A. Griswold, mayor from 1855 to 1856. The opera house opened in 1871.

Frear's Cash Bazaar Building. It is located at the southeast corner of Fulton and Third Streets, replacing the earlier American Hotel (Frear House). The interior stairway is considered a work of art. During the 1950s, radio station WPTR broadcast daily from the mezzanine as Boom Boom Branigan and Paul Flannigan spun out rock-and-roll records. Originally opened in 1897, it is still in use today.

Street Scene Looking South on Third Street from the Market Block. Frear's is on the left. This photograph was taken during the Hudson-Fulton celebration of 1909.

THIRD STREET LOOKING NORTH, INTERSECTION AT BROADWAY (ALBANY STREET UNTIL 1861). Frear's is in the distance. This block is now occupied by the Atrium.

THE *TROY TIMES* BUILDING, C. 1892, ON THE NORTHEAST CORNER OF THIRD AND BROADWAY. The building was erected in 1871 and remodeled six years later due to a fire. The *Troy Times* was taken over by the *Troy Record* in 1935. The site is now occupied by the Atrium.

G.V.S Quackenbush & Co., Department Store, Southeast Corner of Third and Broadway. The store was built in 1855. Quackenbush was the oldest dry goods store in the city. Founded in 1824, it was popular until the 1920s. W.T. Grant occupied it until the 1960s.

The Troy Trust Company, Southwest Corner Broadway and Third Street, Founded in 1901. It first operated in the Ilium building, then moved to this house, the old Dr. Nathan B. Warren residence, and the first floor was remodeled. In 1924 the company remodeled again and took over the entire building. Marine Midland bank building now occupies the site.

KEENAN BUILDING, NORTHWEST CORNER OF BROADWAY AND THIRD STREET, BUILT IN 1882. Early renters included Thomas H. Magill, millinery and fancy goods; Edgar L. Everett's art store; Samuel B. Mount, fur dealer; Theodore A Byram, merchant tailor; Hudson & Smith, general insurance agents; Zeph F. Magill, photographer; George Harrison, farm real estate; and William V. Baker, insurance agent.

LOOKING WEST TOWARDS MONUMENT SQUARE ON BROADWAY FROM THIRD STREET. Mansion House is on the right and Cannon Place is on the left across Second Street. Green building is on the immediate left.

CANNON PLACE, WASHINGTON SQUARE, ERECTED IN 1835 BY LE GRAND CANNON. William H. Frear bought it from Cannon in 1891 and created Frear's Cash Bazaar, the predecessor of his department store on Third and Fulton Streets. Bull's Head Tavern occupied this site from 1806 to 1814.

MANSION HOUSE (FAR RIGHT BUILDING) ON EAST SIDE OF WASHINGTON SQUARE (MONUMENT SQUARE), SOUTHEAST CORNER OF SECOND AND BROADWAY. Built in 1828 by Nathan Warren, it served as an important meeting place for many years. Washington Square was laid out in 1787. The name was changed by the Common Council on September 13, 1818. A marble fountain, 125 feet high with three basins, was erected in 1835. In 1848, a circular fence was built, and after the removal of the fountain, trees were planted by Charles L. Richards. This photograph was taken around 1912 or 1913.

HENDRICK (HENRY) HUDSON HOTEL ON EAST SIDE OF MONUMENT SQUARE. This hotel replaced the Mansion House in 1925. John F. Kennedy and Richard Nixon spoke here in 1960. It now houses offices and a number of high-tech firms. Looking east along Broadway you can see the Keenan and *Troy Times* buildings.

MONUMENT SQUARE, LOOKING WEST. The McCarthy building is in back of the Soldiers and Sailors Monument, built in 1891 to commemorate the soldiers of the U.S. Civil War. The monument is 93 feet high. The "Call to Arms" statue is 13 feet high. Several plaques on the monument depict famous battles and other war related information. Private Daniel Mooney, Company E, Second Regiment N.Y.S. Volunteers was the first Troy soldier to die in the Civil War. The Cannon Place building is to the left.

TROY HOUSE, INTERSECTION OF FIRST AND RIVER STREETS, LOOKING NORTHEAST, C. 1903. Originally, several buildings (Eagle Tavern 1797, Titus's Inn in 1805) were renovated in 1855 to this appearance. In 1905, the house was demolished for the existing hotel building and called "The Rensselaer." In 1924, the name changed to Hotel Troy. It is now housing for seniors.

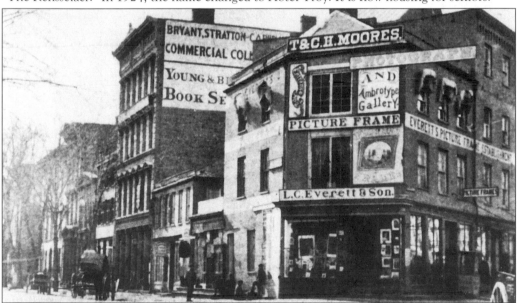

LANE'S ROW, INTERSECTION OF FIRST AND RIVER STREETS, LOOKING SOUTH. Aaron and Derick Lane were successful merchants from Lansingburgh who relocated to Troy. Young & Blake Booksellers and early Bryant & Stratton College were in the building to the left. Young published the first *History of Troy* by Arthur Weise. This area burned in the fire of 1820. The Hall (Rice) building occupies the site today.

HALL BUILDING, SOUTHEAST INTERSECTION OF RIVER AND FIRST STREETS. The building was erected by Benjamin H. Hall in 1871. It replaced Lane's Row. Today it is called the Rice building. This photograph was taken in 1922.

INTERSECTION OF RIVER AND FIRST STREETS LOOKING NORTH TOWARDS MONUMENT SQUARE. Hall (Rice) building is at right. Rensselaer Hotel is just past it on the right. To the left, just past the horse and wagon, are the offices of the *Troy Sentinel* newspaper where *A Visit from St. Nicholas*, better known as *Twas the Night Before Christmas*, was first published on December 23, 1823. This classic was penned by Clement C. Moore, an episcopal minister from New York City and friend of Rev. David Butler of St. Paul's Episcopal Church in Troy. Butler's daughter had the poem printed in Troy.

RIVER STREET LOOKING NORTH FROM THE CORNER OF CONGRESS STREET. The drug firm of John L. Thompson is on the immediate left across River Street and operated in Troy until the 1970s. It began in 1797, on this same site, by Samuel Gale.

NATIONAL CITY BANK, NORTHEAST CORNER OF FIRST AND STATE STREETS. Charles Nalle, a slave, escaped to Troy in 1858 and worked as a coachman until he was arrested on April 27, 1860, under the Fugitive Slave Act. He was turned in by a lawyer from Sand Lake who contacted the slave owner. Nalle was taken here to the U.S. Commissioners Office (second floor) but freed by an angry mob of Trojans who took him to West Troy (Watervliet) where he was captured, but freed again. He spent time hiding in the Albany Pine Barrens and in Amsterdam until his freedom was purchased for $650. He spent his remaining years a free man in Troy. The bank was then the Mutual National Bank of Troy, which began here in 1853.

FEDERAL PERIOD HOME OF THOMAS BUCKLEY ON THE NORTHWEST CORNER OF STATE AND SECOND STREETS. The home was picked up and moved farther west to the alley across the street (back of house sliced off) where it still sits today. The Caldwell Apartment building, Troy's first, was built in its place in 1907.

TROY SAVINGS BANK, NORTHEAST CORNER OF STATE AND SECOND STREETS. It is the oldest existing bank in Troy and was incorporated in 1823. Their first home, the Athenaeum building was built on First Street in 1845–46 and the bank moved here to Second Street in 1875. The famous Music Hall is located here.

GEORGE VAIL HOUSE, NORTHEAST CORNER OF CONGRESS AND FIRST STREETS. This house is now used as the residence of the president of Russell Sage College. George Vale was president of the Merchants and Mechanics' Bank, a successful merchant, a city alderman, a first director of the Rensselaer & Saratoga Railroad, and associate of the Troy Steamboat Company.

THE TROY CLUB, ORGANIZED IN 1867. The club first purchased a clubhouse on the northwest corner of Second and Congress Streets. In 1888, it purchased property on the southwest corner of First and Congress Streets and built this Romanesque-style clubhouse. The clubhouse burned in 1981. This photograph was taken in 1933.

FIRST PRESBYTERIAN CHURCH, SOUTHWEST CORNER OF SEMINARY PARK ALONG FIRST STREET. Erected in 1836, it is now owned by Russell Sage College. It is the oldest church building in the city. It replaced an earlier meetinghouse nearby. The park, 280 by 150 feet between Congress, First, and Second Streets, was given to the village of Troy by Jacob D. Van der Heyden in 1796 for the use as a public square and for a public schoolhouse or academy.

RYNALDO APARTMENT HOUSE, NORTHWEST CORNER OF CONGRESS AND SECOND STREET FACING SEMINARY PARK, C. 1940. The building is now gone having been replaced by housing for Russell Sage students.

SEMINARY PARK AND TROY FEMALE SEMINARY, C. 1890, LOOKING SOUTHWEST. The Female Seminary was created by Emma Willard who believed girls should be taught the same subjects as boys. She opened a school for girls using the old Moulton's Coffeehouse (renovated in 1821, lengthened in 1826, and continually expanded). In 1873, the building was sold to the school trustees by the city. In 1892 the present set of buildings, Gurley Memorial Hall and Anna M. Plum Memorial, were built. In 1895, it changed to the Emma Willard School. Emma Willard School moved to its present location in 1910, and this site became Russell Sage College in 1916. The school still continues with its mission to teach women.

SECOND COURTHOUSE, SOUTHEAST CORNER OF SECOND AND CONGRESS STREETS. The first courthouse was built here in 1794. A jail was in the rear. This courthouse was opened in 1831 and replaced by the present courthouse in 1898.

WILLIAM HOWARD HART MEMORIAL PUBLIC LIBRARY, NORTHEAST CORNER OF FERRY AND SECOND STREETS. The library was built in 1897 as a gift from Mary Lane Hart to the citizens of Troy for her late husband. It has a beautiful interior, and still serves as a public library. It is one of the oldest libraries in the state with its beginning in 1799. In 1820, the library had 687 volumes.

INTERNATIONAL HOTEL, SOUTHEAST CORNER FERRY AND RIVER STREETS, C. 1870. It was built in 1803 as a two-story house for Derick V. Van Der Heyden. The third floor was added in 1831 and called the National Hotel. Aaron Burr was a guest. In 1864, its name changed to the St. Charles, and in 1866 it changed names again to the International. The structure was torn down in 1884 for the new N.Y.S. Armory.

RENSSELAER COUNTY JAIL, NORTHEAST CORNER OF FERRY AND FIFTH AVENUE. The first jail was erected in the rear of the first courthouse in 1795. This jail was built in 1826 and torn down in 1911 for the present jail building, which is being reused for county government offices.

SAMUEL WILSON'S HOUSE, "UNCLE SAM," FERRY STREET ALONG MOUNT IDA, NEAR THE INTERSECTION OF SIXTH STREET. Wilson packed beef for U.S. soldiers near Greenbush, New York (War of 1812). The barrels were labeled U.S., and soldiers and army contractors who knew Wilson referred to them as "Uncle Sam's beef." The house was built in 1793 and was torn down shortly before the nation's Bicentennial celebration in 1976. This photograph was taken c. 1900.

THE TROY DAY HOME, EAST SIDE OF SEVENTH STREET, BETWEEN STATE AND CONGRESS STREETS. The old Tibbits Mansion and lot were purchased in 1861 to be used as a daycare center for working-class children. It was still functioning in the 1960s, and is now a parking lot for the Ned Pattison Government Center.

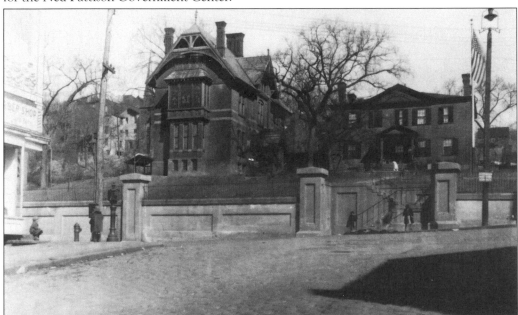

THE DAY HOME AND CHAPEL/SCHOOL. In 1879, E. Thompson Gale erected the chapel and school in honor of his son. Designed by Marcus Cummings, a local architect, about one hundred kids averaged attendance in the 1880s. The retaining wall is still there.

CONGRESS STREET LOOKING WEST. Congress Hall (hotel) is just past the train tunnel abutment to the right. Congress Hall was built in 1848. All of the buildings seen here are gone.

CONGRESS STREET LOOKING EAST. The Fifth Avenue intersection can be seen towards the bottom of this photograph. Most of the buildings seen here are gone. The Day Home, Tibbits Mansion, is at top. The photograph was taken prior to 1879.

RAND'S OPERA HOUSE, C. 1890, NORTHWEST CORNER FOURTH AND CONGRESS STREETS.
This structure was originally built as Rand's Hall. It was enlarged in 1872 for dramatic presentations and known as Rand's Opera House. It opened Monday evening, November 11, 1872, with readings by the internationally famous English actress, Mrs. Scott Siddons, and burned on January 31, 1922.

INTERIOR OF RAND'S OPERA HOUSE AFTER IT WAS REMODELED IN 1888.

CITY HALL, SOUTHEAST CORNER OF STATE AND THIRD STREETS (NOW BARKER PARK). It was originally the town burial ground. More than two hundred graves were relocated to Oakwood and other cemeteries. Designed by Marcus Cummings, Troy City Hall was occupied in October 1876. It burned under suspicious conditions on October 28, 1938.

THIRD STREET LOOKING NORTH FROM THE INTERSECTION OF STATE STREET (CITY HALL). The Arba Reed Fire Station is on the left. St. Paul's Episcopal Church is on the right.

FRIENDS MEETINGHOUSE, C. 1865, SOUTHWEST CORNER OF FOURTH AND STATE STREETS.
In 1806, the Troy Quakers rented the frame building here, then purchased it in 1807.
Enrollment declined and the property sold to the First Unitarian Church in 1874. Torn down
in 1874, the Unitarians built a church a year later. It was sold to St. Anthony's Catholic
Church in 1905.

**ST. ANTHONY'S ROMAN
CATHOLIC CHURCH.**
Purchased from the
Unitarians in 1905, it was
extensively renovated and
reopened May 26, 1907, with
the confirmation of one
hundred Italian children. It
was torn down, but the lot is
still used by the church. New
church is a few yards west in
Barker Park. There were 46
churches in Troy in 1886.

J.H. Warren House, 68 Fourth Street c. 1886. This is the present location of the post office. J.H. Warren was one of the owners of Fuller, Warren & Co., a foundry that made world-famous "Stewart" brand cast-iron stoves.

U.S. Government Building (post office), Northeast Corner Broadway and Fourth Streets. Federal Court, Civil Service, IRS, and Army and Navy recruiters shared this building with the post office. Built in 1894, it was replaced in 1936 by a WPA project.

W. & L.E. Gurley Building, Northeast Corner of Fulton Street and Fifth Avenue. Built after the fire of 1862, Gurley's is world famous for surveyors transits and scientific instruments to this day.

North Side of Fulton Street at the Intersection of Fifth Avenue. The third building on the right (northwest corner) is the Fifth Avenue Hotel. The building on the left, 562 Fulton, held Edmund J. Cridge who made stove patterns. The middle building is Wheeler & Wilson Manufacturing Company who made sewing machines that became the standard for collar, cuff, and shirt makers in Troy. These buildings are gone. The Gurley building can be seen at the extreme right.

THE TROY RECORD BUILDING, SOUTHEAST CORNER OF BROADWAY AND FIFTH AVENUE.
Built in 1909, the *Morning Record* and the *Evening Record* were published here, now simply *The Record*. In the 1880s, there were 18 newspapers and periodicals published in Troy. The Troy Record began in 1896 with the morning paper.

THE ILIUM BUILDING, NORTHEAST CORNER OF FULTON AND FOURTH STREETS. This building still houses a mix of shops on the street level, and offices above.

FOURTH STREET LOOKING NORTH ABOVE FULTON STREET TOWARDS FRANKLIN SQUARE IN 1913. All of the buildings on the left and center are gone. Flood waters from the March 1913 flood can be seen in the foreground.

FRANKLIN SQUARE LOOKING SOUTH. River Street is to the right and Fourth Street is to the left. All that remains are the buildings on the east side of Fourth Street (left). Once a thriving part of Troy, the entire area was razed during urban renewal of the 1960s and 1970s.

FRANKLIN SQUARE LOOKING NORTH TOWARD CHATHAM SQUARE C. 1910. This was a very busy part of Troy. Most of the buildings you see in this picture are gone.

FRANKLIN SQUARE LOOKING SOUTH. This image was taken during the 1960s, shortly before urban renewal tore down the square.

MANUFACTURERS NATIONAL BANK, LANDMARK OF CHATHAM SQUARE, INTERSECTION OF KING AND RIVER STREETS. The bank opened in this former train station in 1856 (train station in 1845). It was organized as the Manufacturers Bank of Troy in 1852. It moved to its new building at the southeast corner of Grand and Fourth in 1922, which included a shooting gallery!

RENSSELAER & SARATOGA RAILROAD BRIDGE, WEST SIDE OF CHATHAM SQUARE. On May 10, 1862, a locomotive on the bridge, over the Hudson River, started a fire. The flames spread rapidly by wind; the fire destroyed 507 buildings in downtown Troy as far east as Eighth Street. Only five lives were lost, but it was Troy's worst fire. Fires in 1820 and 1854 were also costly, destroying much of the commercial district closer to the river.

RIVER STREET LOOKING NORTH FROM CHATHAM SQUARE. Some of the buildings in the center, which includes the Fitzgerald Brewery Company, are gone. The trolley was headed to Albia.

CHATHAM SQUARE LOOKING WEST OVER THE BRIDGE. This large gun was made at the Watervliet Arsenal across the river and was being taken to the Troy Union Station for shipment probably to a war theater during the First World War.

THE GREEN ISLAND BRIDGE OPENED AT CHATHAM SQUARE IN 1925.

AERIAL VIEW OF DOWNTOWN TROY. This image shows Chatham and Franklin Squares, Market Block, and much of the core business district now gone as a result of urban renewal (removal) of the 1960s and 1970s. The Green Island bridge is to the right.

Two

TROY'S INDUSTRIES AND MERCHANTS

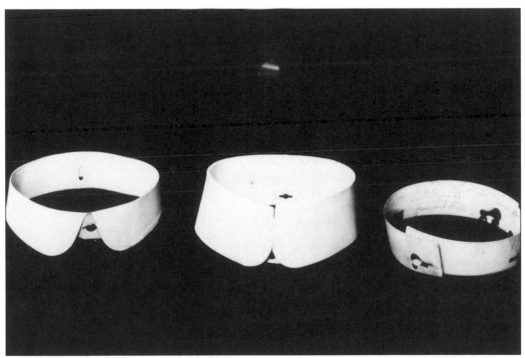

PAPER, CELLULOID, AND STEEL COLLAR. Mrs. Hannah Lord Montague reportedly made the first detachable shirt collar at her home at 139 Third Street in Troy around 1827. The collar, cuff, and shirt industry became one of Troy's leading industries and the city became known as "The Collar City." By 1925, out of every one hundred dozen collars worn, more than 90 dozen were made in Troy by 15,000 workers, mostly women. Troy was making a million collars a day and half a million shirts a week.

THE CLEMINSHAW BUILDING (FAR RIGHT), 421–423 RIVER STREET C. 1904. In 1884, H.C. Curtis and Charles Cleminshaw formed the H.C. Curtis & Co., linen collar and cuff manufacturers. Their collars and cuffs were nationally known. They merged with the International Shirt & Collar Company on May 30, 1906. John Consalus at 417–419 River Street (center building) was a wool dealer who moved to this building in 1871, carrying on the tradition that started with Hiram Herrington in 1843 at 273 River. The Aird-Don building is to the left at 409–415 River Street.

EARL & WILSON COLLARS AND CUFFS, SOUTHWEST CORNER SEVENTH AVENUE AND BROADWAY. The company began at 5 Union, in 1867, and moved to this building in 1876. The E&W trademark was well known around the country. This entire section of Seventh Avenue in Troy is gone.

MILLER, HALL, & HARTWELL BUILDINGS, MAKERS OF SHIRTS, CUFFS, AND COLLARS, AT 347–357 RIVER STREET. This was one of the oldest and largest shirt makers. The first building was built in 1880, the second in 1891. The firm of Miller, Hall, & Hartwell formed in 1884. Hall & Hartwell & Co., seen here, was incorporated in 1923.

GEORGE P. IDE & CO., COLLARS, CUFFS AND SHIRTS, 506 RIVER STREET. The company formed in 1882, but began as Ide & Ford (S.V.R. Ford) in 1865. This large building was erected in 1907. The smaller one to the left was a storeroom. Fitzgerald Brewery is at the far end.

CLUETT, PEABODY & CO. RIVER STREET. These buildings were built in 1881, 1884, and 1890, and became the largest collar factories in the world. In 1916, the three buildings were remolded into one. Arrow shirts were made here until the early 1980s.

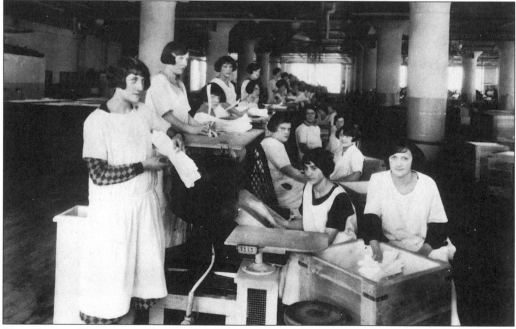

THE COLLAR DAMPENING DIVISION OF CLUETT, PEABODY DURING THE 1920s.

MT. IDA WOOL COTTON MILLS, 1840. In later years Troy Shirt Waist Company, Trojan Cloth Manufacturing Company, and Browning, King, & Company operated out of these buildings. They were demolished in the early 1980s.

MOUNT IDA FALLS (POESTENKILL FALLS), LOCATED ON THE POESTENKILL. This was a popular place for tourists and picnickers during the 19th century. Just below it were many waterpowered industries, starting with the sawmill of Jan Barentsen Wemp, as early as 1667. This photograph was taken on May 26, 1885.

WATER-POWERED MILLS. In 1840, Benjamin Marshall constructed a 600-foot waterpower tunnel that allowed several mills and factories to develop and operate up until the 1960s. Here the Griswold Wire Works operated from 1879 to 1911. Paper, cotton, and metal items were made here. Only foundation ruins exist today along this stream.

TOMPKINS MACHINE SHOP, 1889, AT THE FOOT OF CONGRESS STREET NEAR GRISWOLD WIRE. This company made knitting goods machinery. It was built in 1850 and called the Empire Machine Company. Clark Tompkins invented the upright rotary knitter.

THE WYANTSKILL. This was the other stream in south Troy that powered Troy industries. These buildings, on the north bank, were part of the Albany Iron Works. This company made the plates for the iron-clad Civil War ship the *Monitor*, which helped turn the war in the favor of the North.

TROY IRON AND STEEL COMPANY ON THE SOUTH SIDE OF THE WYANTSKILL, C. 1885. This set of buildings was part of the Albany Iron Works. Wrought iron was made here in 1839. In 1849, the steam mill was built.

THE BESSEMER STEEL WORKS, 1884. John A. Griswold, John F. Winslow, and Alexander L. Holley purchased the old flour mill site of Thomas L. Witbeck (1796) on the bank of the Hudson River south of the Wyantskill. They built this 2 1/2-ton plant that made the first Bessemer steel in the United States on February 16, 1865.

THE BURDEN IRON COMPANY, LOWER WORKS. In 1822, Henry Burden became superintendent of the Troy Iron and Nail Factory. He soon invented a wrought nail and spike machine, counter-sunk railroad spikes machines, and a horseshoe-making machine, which made him famous, and other patented inventions. In 1838–39, he constructed the largest waterwheel in the country. During the Civil War, his firm supplied most of the horseshoes for the northern army. Burden's became one of Troy's biggest iron companies. All that exists today are the office building and ladle car.

THE FAMOUS BURDEN IRON WHEEL, UPPER WORKS. Built in 1838–39, it was 60 feet in diameter, 22 feet wide, with 36 buckets, 6 feet 3 inches deep, that provided output of 1,200 horsepower. It was called "the Niagara of water wheels." It has been thought to be the impetus for the invention of the Ferris Wheel, created by bridge builder George Ferris, an RPI graduate. The first Ferris Wheel debuted at the 1893 World's Columbian Exposition in Paris. It, too, had 36 "buckets" (seats).

MARSHALL FOUNDRY, IDA HILL, OFF CONGRESS STREET. William P. and Warren T. Kellogg manufactured hardware items like currycombs, portable forges, boring, and mortising machines in his foundry on the banks of the Poestenkill during the 1870s. This photograph was taken *c.* 1870.

FULLER & WARREN CLINTON STOVE WORKS. Just north of Burden's lower works, 1,200 workers on 6 acres made 60,000 stoves annually, making "Stewart" brand stoves known worldwide. Stove making on this site started as early as 1846. The few remaining buildings are being torn down in 1998. Stoves were made in Troy in 1821 and at least 23 companies were making them in 1875.

TAKING THE IRON FROM THE CUPOLA (FURNACE). Stove workers from Fuller and Warren are getting ready to pour iron into the molds for stoves.

HOYT & WYNKOOP, NICKEL PLATERS AND IRON FOUNDERS, 1885. Located on Spring Avenue, the company was formed by James B. Hoyt and George W. Wynkoop in 1875 and employed 90 workmen.

ROBINSON, CHURCH & CO., 189–201 RIVER STREET, WHOLESALE DRUGGISTS. In 1879, Daniel Robinson, Charles R. Church, and John A. Robinson formed this company, succeeding various incarnations of the company since 1805.

JOSEPH CHUCKROW SONS, 93 RIVER STREET. Fresh chickens, butter, and eggs were available here for many years. During the 1960s, you could see trucks of chickens heading to the loading docks to meet their fate. Now the firm is in nearby Latham.

HARVEY & EDDY, WHOLESALE GROCERS AT 277 RIVER STREET. D.H. Harvey and C.G. Eddy continued the business started by Robert Harvey & Brother at 355 Fulton in 1873.

SQUIRES, SHERRY, & GALUSHA, GROCERS AT 279 RIVER STREET. Starkweather, Allen, & Baker, merchants at 237 River, were in the left building in this image. The J.W. Warren building is on the right, c. 1876.

J.M. WARREN & CO., 245–247 RIVER STREET. This was one of Troy's largest hardware stores. Built in 1870, Warren's sold nationwide until the building was burned and torn down in the 1970s. Founded in 1809 as Hart & Nazro, the original site was where the Rice building is now standing. Warren incorporated in 1887.

KENNEDY & MURPHY BREWERS. This was the first established brewery and was located on Ferry Street east of Fifth Avenue (near the Ferry Street Tunnel). A brewery by Charles Hurstfield, Thomas Trenor, and successors started here in 1809 and operated until 1867 when William Kennedy and Edward Murphy Jr. purchased the property. It was then called the Excelsior Brewery, which was gone by the 1930s.

THE STANTON BREWERY, 1428–1440 FIFTH AVENUE. It was started in 1817 by Abram Nash. John Stanton took over in 1880. Stanton Brewery made ale and porter until the 1960s. The site is now used by the Italian Community Center.

THE GARRYOWEN BREWERY, BUILT DURING 1877 TO 1881 ON RIVER STREET BETWEEN HUTTON AND HOOSICK STREETS. In 1866, Fitzgerald Brothers (Michael, John, and Edmund) began making beer here. In 1885, upon the death of John, the named changed to Fitzgerald Brothers. They made beer into the 1960s. In 1880, there were nine Troy breweries making over 205,000 barrels of beer. There are none today of this scale, but there is a brewpub making original beer again in Troy, not too far from this site.

REARDON & ENNIS, 311 RIVER STREET. They were dealers in stoves and ranges and made galvanized iron cornices and tinware. John Reardon and George H. Ennis continued the business started here by E. Bussey & Co. in 1863.

55

BURTIS & MANN, 231 RIVER STREET. O.F. Burtis and H.R. Mann formed this company in 1883 succeeding the business of Potter & Co. and H.S. Church. They made stoves at the J. Gould Foundry on the southwest corner of North Third and North Streets. Their salesroom was here at 231 River. This photograph was taken *c.* 1880.

FEDERAL AND SIXTH AVENUE INTERSECTION. Teddy & Neil Grill (Theodore Morsello owner) at 561 Federal Street operated during the 1930s. Next to it is Wager's Ice Cream factory, 551–557 Federal, makers of Wager's and Duke's Ice Cream. School field trips (and free ice cream) were common in the 1950s. This entire block is gone. Notice the train tracks.

NIAGARA HUDSON COKE COMPANY. Hudson Valley Coke and Products Corporation was started in 1924 at the old Rensselaer Iron Works and Troy Steel and Iron Company, to make coke, coke byproducts, and coal gas. Created by members of the old Burden Iron Company, the company was short-lived.

WHEELER BROTHERS IRON AND BRASS FOUNDRY. A foundryman pours brass at the foundry atop Mount Olympus in 1989. This foundry went out of business shortly afterwards. Only one remaining Troy iron foundry, Ross Valve, makes iron the old-fashioned way.

TROY RIVERFRONT FROM THE CONGRESS STREET BRIDGE, LOOKING SOUTH. This river view shows oil barges ready for filling. Center Island, once the home of an iron foundry, became a point of gas and oil storage.

STODDARD & BURTON, DRUGGISTS FROM 1855 TO 1872, 89 CONGRESS. In the same building here was Zimri Burton, harness maker at 91 Congress, and Henry Adams, grocer at 86 Congress. This is the southwest corner of Congress and Third, 86–91 Congress Street, *c.* 1862.

MENEELY BELL FOUNDRY.
The first Troy bell foundry
was erected by Julius Hanks in
1825 on the present site of the
Gurley building, Fulton Street
and Fifth Avenue. The
Clinton H. Meneely Bell
Company began on the east
side of River Street between
Washington and Adams
Street and used part of the
bell foundry erected in 1869
by Clinton H. Meneely and
George H. Kimberly (Meneely
& Kimberly) until they
dissolved in 1879. In 1912,
they cast a 10,000-pound
church bell for the Church of
Christ in San Diego. Their
bells are world famous for
their sound.

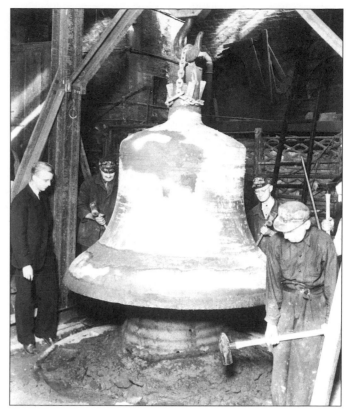

**MICHAEL MAHONY
ARCHITECTURAL
IRON WORKS AND
FOUNDRY.** Mahony
was originally teamed
with Calvin Link in
1870, making cast-
iron storefronts under
the name Link &
Mahony, and located
on Hollow Road
(Spring Avenue). The
new foundry was built
on the northwest
corner of Liberty and
Fifth Avenue (now
Lusco Paper Supply)
in 1878. That same
year Mahony went on
his own and
continued making
iron storefronts, and
eventually boilers into
the early 20th century.

CHARLES F. FREIHOFER BAKERY. While located in Lansingburgh, this bakery started in 1913 by Charles C., Edwin, and Frank Freihofer and delivered fresh bread, cookies, and baked goods by horse and buggy until the 1960s. You could hear the clap-clap of the horses at 3 a.m. while deliveries were being made. Still in business, although now owned by a national chain, they make the best chocolate-chip cookies in the world.

ROSS VALVE. The last of the working Troy iron foundries, Ross Valve, 6 Oakwood Avenue, was founded in 1879 and moved to this building in 1893. It continues to make water and pressure regulating valves for worldwide use. After receiving a patent for a "fluid pressure regulator" in 1879, George Ross founded Ross Valve and incorporated in 1917. In the early 1900s more than eight hundred valves controlled New York City's water supply. They still use the casting methods used for hundreds of years.

Three

TRANSPORTATION AND MOVEMENT

COACH IN FRONT OF THE CHARLES W. FREAR HOUSE AT 65 SECOND STREET IN 1890. The Hart Cluett Mansion, now Rensselaer County Historical Society, is at right.

AVERILL PARK TROLLEY. The Troy & New England Railway was promoted by Troy and Sand Lake business people. This line was constructed in 1894–95 from Albia to Averill Park, where a resort community developed. James K. Averill was the chief promoter (he owned large tracts of land in Sand Lake) and was made the company's first president. This company was absorbed by the Delaware & Hudson Company in 1906.

TROY-LANSINGBURG COMPANY, WATERFORD TO IRON WORKS LINE. Iron Works was a train station near the Burden Iron Works. The first railway in Troy was the Troy & Lansingburgh Horse Railroad. A single track was laid through River, Adams, and Second Streets to a point on the Greenbush highway near a bridge over the Wyantskill. The first car, called "The Red Line," began on August 30, 1861. The line extended to Waterford in 1862.

TROLLEY-CAR SCENE. The trolley system took you anywhere you wanted to go in Troy. Here a trolley rolls through Franklin Square towards Fourth Street.

CANAL BOATS READY FOR MOVING INTO THE ERIE CANAL, AT WEST TROY, KNOWN AS THE WATERVLIET CUT. Canal boats were a popular way to travel not only for business and trade, but for pleasure as well. The Erie Canal cut emptied here into the Hudson River, before it continued into the city of Albany to the north, the terminus of the canal. Many of the packet boats were made nearby by Matton Ship Yards, who also made tugboats into the 1970s.

STEAM-POWERED FERRYBOAT. Troy was first known as Ashley's Ferry, for the ferry crossing near what is Ferry Street today to Gibbonsville (Watervliet) in 1798. That year Mahlon Taylor started a ferry at the foot of Washington Street. Four ferries operated in Troy. Broadway to the south end of Green Island was a route, too. First as flat-bottomed boats polled to the opposite shore, later horse-powered (real horses, that is), and then steam powered (1826). Douw Street, Troy, and Tibbits Street, Green Island, were terminals for the steam ferry built after the construction of the Federal Dam. In 1911 the ferryboat went over the dam killing three people and was discontinued. These landing sites were then used by steam-powered ferryboats like this one for years.

STEAMBOAT LANDINGS AT THE BOTTOM OF STATE STREET, OR BROADWAY. They were a boarding area for steamers that were owned by local companies. This view before 1862 shows the bridge to Green Island, and Starbuck Iron Foundry on Center Island. The Utica steamboat went to NYC beginning in 1837.

OLDEST STEAMBOAT IN THE WORLD. The *Norwich*, built in 1836, is seen here in 1909.

W.H. FREAR, TROY MERCHANT. He owned Frear's Cash Bazaar and had his own boat named for him.

THE CITY OF TROY. On April 1, 1876, it launched and arrived at steamboat landing at Broadway on June 15. The boat was owned by the Citizen's Steamboat Company of Troy, organized in 1871. The steamer was 300 feet long, 70 feet breath, and weighed 1,650 tons. It had 112 staterooms, 40 ladies' cabin berths, and 210 cabin berths for men. It took ten hours to go from Troy to New York City, making daily trips (except Saturday). It burned on April 1, 1907, 31 years after it launched.

THE SARATOGA. The second steamer of the Citizen's Steamboat Company of Troy was launched on March 26, 1877, and arrived in Troy on June 13. It collided with the *Adirondack* opposite Saugerties Creek on October 13, 1906, and grounded on Hog's Back Reef. Three hundred passengers were aboard. Two people died, including a former general manager of the Citizen's Line, and ten people were injured. This boat was 300 feet long, 68 feet wide, and weighed 1,550 tons. It had one more stateroom than the *City of Troy.*

THE *BELLE HORTON*, BUILT IN 1880. It was also owned by the Citizen's Steamboat Company of Troy and was used for excursions and as a tender for the larger boats.

THE *J.G. SANDERS*. The Albany and Troy Steamboat Company owned this ship. It shuttled between the two cities and boarded at the State Street landing in Troy and Maiden Lane in Albany.

STEAMER AT WORK. Steamers were also used as freight and work boats. Here a specially equipped steamer takes train cars across the river.

THE TROJAN, BUILT IN 1909 BY THE HUDSON NAVIGATION COMPANY. Fares to New York City were about $1. The *Trojan* and *Rensselaer*, their other steamer, made overnight daily trips without intermediate stops. They served both passengers and freight.

THE *TROJAN* AND THE *HALF MOON* (REPLICA) DURING THE 1909 HUDSON-FULTON CELEBRATION HELD FROM SEPTEMBER 25 TO OCTOBER 9. The final day of the event was called Troy Day since Troy was the head of Hudson River navigation.

THE FEDERAL DAM AND SLOOP LOCK, BUILT IN 1823, OPPOSITE MIDDLEBURG STREET, A BLOCK SOUTH OF THE PRESENT DAM. The dam was 1,100 feet long and 9 feet high. The lock was 31 feet high and 114 feet long.

THE TROY UNION RAILROAD STATION, C. 1863. The first station was built in 1854, but burned in the 1862 fire. It had a great oak arch of 150 feet. The station was rebuilt immediately with a steel arched roof.

THE STATION AROUND 1870. It was taken down in 1899 for a brand-new station built in 1903, with subways to the tracks. Troy Union Railroad was jointly controlled by Rensselaer & Saratoga, Troy & Schenectady, Troy & Greenbush, and Troy & Boston railroads.

Entrance to Richards & Jordan's Baggage Express (cabs and carriages) at the front of the Troy Union Railroad Station, Union Street Side, c. 1890.

The "Chippewa." It is ready to move from the south end of the train station, looking east up Broadway. The main building of Rensselaer Polytechnic Institute, built after the Troy fire of 1862, can be seen at the top of Broadway and Eighth. The building burned in 1904.

THE "COMMODORE VANDERBILT" AT THE TROY UNION RAILROAD STATION, LOOKING
WEST ON FULTON, C. 1865. The Tremont House is to the right and was founded in 1855.
Known as the Everett House in the 1890s, it is now a parking lot. The Gurley building is next
to it, and the Earl & Wilson, Collar and Cuff Manufacturers are next to the train station, now
owned by Gurley. Notice the picture of Mr. Vanderbilt on the headlight.

"JAMES M. MARVIN," A RENSSELAER & SARATOGA RAILROAD ENGINE BUILT IN 1867 BY
THE SCHENECTADY LOCOMOTIVE WORKS. This railroad company was incorporated in 1832
and began building its road the following year. In 1835, the first car crossed to Troy. Until 1853,
the cars were drawn by horse across the Rensselaer & Saratoga bridge (Green Island bridge)
through River Street to offices at 10 First Street (just south of the Troy Hotel). That bridge
burned in 1862 and destroyed most of downtown Troy. This photograph was taken c. 1865.

72

THE "E. THOMPSON GALE" OF THE RENSSELAER & SARATOGA RAILROAD. The engine was built in 1869. E. Thompson Gale was president of the Union National Bank of Troy, created in 1865. He remained president until 1885 when he retired due to poor health.

THE "PONY," AN ENGINE OF THE TROY & BOSTON RAILROAD, C. 1865. The T&B Railroad was responsible for the construction of the famous Hoosac Tunnel, a 5-mile underground tunnel connecting the east and west branches of the railroad through the Berkshire Mountains. At the time, it was the longest tunnel in the United States. The first train from Troy to Boston left on July 17, 1875, at 7 a.m. and arrived in Boston at 2:30 p.m.

TROY & BOSTON RAILROAD YARDS WITH MOUNT OLYMPUS IN THE BACKGROUND IN 1860, VIEW FROM EIGHTH STREET. This railroad incorporated in 1849 and the road formed in 1851. The first train came to Troy on June 28, 1852. This area became the freight yards of the Boston & Maine Railroad.

SAME VIEW WITH LOCOMOTIVE, THE WALLOOMSAC OF THE TROY & BOSTON RAILROAD, C. 1865. An engine house and roundhouse were located here in 1858. The roundhouse is still there and owned by a plumbing concern.

74

THE "ALVAH CROCKER" OF THE TROY & BOSTON RAILROAD, C. 1890.

THE FITCHBURG RAILROAD. It was consolidated with the Troy & Boston Railroad in 1887. On May 2, 1887, the Fitchburg Railroad Company took possession of the Troy & Boston Railroad. The Fitchburg Railroad was absorbed by the Boston & Maine Railroad in 1905.

Engine #3, the Little Engine That Could! This Burden Iron Company steam engine no doubt pulled the Ladle Car full of molten metal to various locations at the plant for processing. It was built in 1906.

Engine #4 of the Burden Iron Company, Built in 1907. It followed the footsteps of Engine #3.

SIXTH AVENUE AND THE MAIN LINE, LOOKING NORTH TOWARDS THE TRAIN STATION.
This image was taken just before the Sixth Avenue (Ferry Street) Tunnel, around 1899. Notice
the switching station. A man had control of hundreds of levers to make sure trains did not
collide. Also, notice that people lived right along the tracks.

THE MAIN LINE LOOKING SOUTH INTO THE SIXTH AVENUE OR FERRY STREET TUNNEL IN
1913. The Congress Hotel is at top right. The tunnel goes through Congress Street and exits at
Ferry Street. The tracks are now a car road, which runs up to Congress burying the tunnel that
is still there. All the houses on both sides are gone.

THE TROY UNION RAILROAD STATION. The old one was torn down in 1899 to make room for this brand new station that opened in August 1903. It had subways to the trains. It was torn down in 1958 for no good reason—a parking lot.

UNION STREET ENTRANCE TO THE TROY UNION RAILROAD STATION.

INTERIOR OF THE TROY UNION STATION. Notice the steps to the right that lead down to the subway that brought you under the tracks and up to the trains on the other side. The Union Street entrance and ticket booth are on the left. This photograph was taken *c.* 1920.

ENGINE #3581 OF THE NEW YORK CENTRAL READY TO MOVE NORTH AT THE TROY UNION STATION. The Troy & Schenectady and Troy & Greenbush Railroads became part of The New York Central. The Troy & Saratoga Railroad became part of the Delaware & Hudson lines. Seventh and Eighth Streets can be seen in the background.

THE TROY AIRPORT. Yes, Troy had an airport south of the Griswold Heights area. It went out of business in the 1960s. This photograph was taken in 1925.

THE GENERAL TIRE "SKY FLEET" PARKED AT THE TROY AIRPORT IN 1925.

AUTOMOBILES. Trojans had no problem taking to the "horse-less carriage."

NOR DID COMMERCIAL ESTABLISHMENTS. This is Frear's Department Store delivery truck. This truck delivered upholstery and carpets.

THE CHANGING FACES OF TRANSPORTATION. Wagons and trolleys gave way to automobiles and bus traffic during the 1930s. The last trolley ran in Troy in 1933. Both views are looking north into River Street from the Market Block. Today this view is only a memory captured in photographs. The entire block was torn down during the late 1960s and early 1970s in a massive urban renewal project. The photograph above, used as the cover for this book, was taken in 1905.

Four

INSTITUTIONS

CHARITABLE, EDUCATIONAL, RELIGIOUS, AND CIVIC

THE "TOWERS OF TROY." This view looking northeast shows the towers of Troy University built in 1856 on Great Lot A, on Eight Street (now RPI). On September 8, 1858, the first term began with 60 students. Only four years later, in October 1862, the building was sold under bankruptcy proceedings. This photograph was taken *c.* 1890s.

ST. JOSEPH'S PROVINCIAL SEMINARY. Troy University was sold to Rev. Peter Havermans of St. Mary's Roman Catholic Church on December 6, 1862. In October 1864, it opened with 60 students. By 1886, 470 priests were ordained. In 1908, it was purchased by the Sisters of St. Joseph as a Provincial House and Novitiate. The building is now gone.

THE ORIGINAL RENSSELAER POLYTECHNIC INSTITUTE (RPI), THE RENSSELAER SCHOOL. Founded in 1824 by Amos Eaton and Stephen Van Rensselaer, the patroon, it was opened on Monday, January 25, 1825 in this building, the old Farmer's Bank building on the northeast corner of River and Middleburg Streets. RPI is one of the great engineering schools and after 175 years, it still is one of the top rated colleges in the country.

THE TROY ACADEMY, ON THE NORTHWEST CORNER OF SEVENTH AND STATE STREETS, INCORPORATED IN 1834. This building was built in 1863 (original burned in the 1862 fire). In 1837, N.Y.S. Legislature passed a law to unite it with the Rensselaer School. The new Rensselaer Institute would be experimental science and the Academy for Classical Literature. While it never happened, Rensselaer changed its name to institute, and many of the academy's teachers were also Rensselaer teachers, and graduates went to the institute. During the 1850s, it was known as the Institute Training School. Taken over by the city for the Fire Alarm and Police Signaling buildings (still there), it was torn down in 1923.

VIEW OF RENSSELAER POLYTECHNIC INSTITUTE SHOWING THE RPI APPROACH TO THE RIGHT AND THE EPISCOPAL CHURCH HOME NEXT TO IT, BUILT IN 1873.

CATHOLIC CENTRAL HIGH SCHOOL. It was erected in 1868 as the Troy Hospital and run by the Sisters of Charity. In 1924, it became Catholic Central High School taught by sisters from St. Joseph and Sisters of Mercy. It is now West Hall, RPI. This photograph was taken in 1931.

RUSSELL SAGE COLLEGE, SEMINARY PARK, BETWEEN CONGRESS AND FERRY STREETS. On the site of Troy Female Seminary and Emma Willard School, Russell Sage College was formed in 1916 and continues today to teach primarily women.

HOUSE OF GOOD SHEPHERD, 1933. Located on the south side of People's Avenue and east of Ninth Street, it was built in 1886. The facility cared for young girls.

THE ATHENAEUM BUILDING. It was erected in 1845 by the Troy Savings Bank, which moved to the new and present Savings Bank building on the northeast corner of State and Second in 1875. The YMCA building is to the left, erected in 1905. They were both torn down in recent years for parking.

MARSHALL INFIRMARY AND RENSSELAER COUNTY LUNATIC ASYLUM, 1937, EAST SIDE OF LINDEN AVENUE NEAR PAWLING AVENUE. Built in 1850 by Benjamin Marshall, who originally wanted it for indigent workmen, it was used for sick people who could not afford medical care. In 1859 the county built a three-story insane asylum, followed in 1861 by another. The original buildings were torn down. The site is now a housing development.

TROY HIGH SCHOOL, FIFTH AVENUE JUST SOUTH OF BROADWAY (NOW PARKING LOT FOR TROY RECORD). It was built in 1898 and first occupied in 1901. It became the Central Grammar School in 1917 and School 5 later. In 1963 the school was torn down.

ST. PETER'S ACADEMY, FIFTH AVENUE NEAR HOOSICK STREET. St. Peter's School became chartered as an academy in 1889. St. Peter's Roman Catholic Church founded it.

CENTRAL SCHOOL OF TROY. Located on the southeast corner of State and Seventh Avenue, the school opened in 1913. The old high school (previous page) was converted to the Central Grammar School and the Classical and Vocational High Schools were combined into this new building as the new Troy High School. During the 1950s, it became School 5. It is now the Rensselaer County Office building.

ST. PAUL'S EPISCOPAL CHURCH, NORTHEAST CORNER OF STATE AND THIRD STREETS. Built in 1828, the interior was redone by the Tiffany Studios before 1900.

MATTHIAS VAN DER HEYDEN'S HOUSE, CORNER OF RIVER AND DIVISION STREETS. It was built in 1752 and demolished in 1886. The house was the first brick building erected within the city limits. Van der Heyden was one of the founding fathers of Troy. Matthias, Jacob D., and Jacob I. Van Der Heyden's farmlands became what is now the city of Troy.

THE GARDNER EARL MEMORIAL CHAPEL AND CREMATORIUM IN 1891. Located in Oakwood Cemetery (created in 1849), the crematorium was built in 1888–89 by William and Hannah M. Earl in memory of their son. It still serves both purposes.

EMMA WILLARD SCHOOL, OFF PAWLING AVENUE. Moved from Seminary Park to East Side in 1910, the school still operates as a private school teaching girls, grades 9–12.

CATHOLIC ORPHAN ASYLUM. It was erected in 1868 on the east side of Eighth Street between Hutton and Hoosick Streets.

CONVENT OF THE GOOD SHEPHERD ON PEOPLE'S AVENUE.

LUNCH TIME. Not exactly a civic institution, but for those who grew up eating at Hot Dog Charlie's or the Famous Lunch they ARE institutions—and still serving. The Famous Lunch opened in 1932. Their hot dogs have been flown to Moscow and many parts of the United States. There are some things a Trojan needs to have no matter where they are. Both Hot Dog Charlie's and the Famous Lunch were started by Greek immigrants and continue as family businesses. Other notable old time eating traditions include the South End Tavern, Manory's, and Rotondi's. This photograph was taken in 1971. The two buildings at right are now gone.

THE TROY HOSPITAL (ST. MARY'S) IN 1945. It was originally organized by Fr. Peter Havermans and called St. Mary's. When the work of the old hospital at Eighth Street outgrew its quarters, they built this site on Oakwood Avenue in 1914. When it opened on September 29, 17 nuns comprised the hospital staff.

The Second Arba Read Fire House, Northwest Corner of State and Third. It was erected in 1875. This volunteer group became the city's first official fire company in February 1860. There were several volunteer fire departments in Troy before they were finally abolished in 1923. Arba Read Station #2, shown here, was built in 1875. In 1885 the Arba Read Steamer Company was formed as a social club and met above the first engine house next to this one. Arba Read was the first president of the Manufacturers Bank of Troy. He also was a principle in what later became the Kennedy and Murphy Brewery in 1856 and was mayor of Troy between 1858 and 1860.

Jason C. Osgood Steam Fire Engine Company No. 3., Southwest Corner of Adams and Second Streets. Built in 1865–66, the company was formed when the Niagara Engine Company No. 7 was discontinued.

Troy Fire Department, Hugh Rankin #2. The Eagle Engine Company No. 10 changed their name to Steam Fire Engine Company No. 2, and then attached the name Hugh Rankin Truck No. 2. They became the first paid company of the Troy Fire Department in 1907. This house on 134 Second Street was built in 1885. By 1924, the fire department was completely motorized. The central Firehouse on State and Sixth Avenue was put in operation in 1925.

Farnam Steamer No. 5 at Work. F.W. Farnam Steam Fire Engine Company No. 5 was organized in 1871 from members of the Lafayette Engine Company No. 10. Both steamers used by the company were made by L. Button & son of Waterford in 1871 and 1885. Their engine house was on the south side of Congress Street.

TROJAN HOOK AND LADDER COMPANY #3. Organized in 1835, it occupied this two-story firehouse on the east side of Franklin Square in 1865.

CHILD'S STEAMER. It is at work on the Draper Cordage Works fire. This may have been William H. Draper, maker of fish and chalk lines and braid wire picture cord at 652–654 River Street. His father began the company in 1865.

Five

PEOPLE AND EVENTS

THE ERECTION OF THE SOLDIERS AND
SAILORS MONUMENT IN WASHINGTON
SQUARE, NOW MONUMENT SQUARE, IN 1891.
It is 93 feet high. The bronze Call to Arms
statute on top is 13 feet high. It was built to
honor the veterans of Rensselaer County.

HUDSON-FULTON CELEBRATION (TOP AND BOTTOM). These Trojans are enjoying the celebration that encompassed the whole Hudson Valley from September 25 to October 9, 1909. The last day was called Troy Day. A large flotilla that included the steamboats *Trojan* and *Rensselaer* escorted the Hudson-Fulton fleet, which included replicas of the *Half Moon* and *Clermont*, the first steamboat on the Hudson. It was topped off with fireworks from the Watervliet Arsenal.

THE PUBLIC MARKET. There were three public markets: Fulton Market at Fulton and River, North Market at Federal Street, and South or Washington Market on the northwest corner of Second and Divisions Streets. This public market was located at Fourth and Division Streets.

PRESIDENT VISITS. Pres. William Howard Taft came to Troy during the Hudson-Fulton celebration in 1909. He is shown here seated next to Gov. Charles Evans Hughes. Taft also visited Cluett, Peabody & Co. while in the city.

BUFFALO BILL AND CRAZY HORSE IN PARADE. P.T. Barnum came to town in 1895. The Gaiety Theater was at 405 River Street and opened in the fall of 1888.

THE JULY 4, 1893 PARADE AT THE MARKET BLOCK, LOOKING NORTH DOWN RIVER STREET. Trojans have always loved a parade. The Boardman building is on the right.

ANOTHER PARADE. It is marching south through Franklin Square on River Street.

MILITARY PARADE NORTH ON THIRD STREET NEAR BROADWAY INTERSECTION. Quackenbush Department Store is on the left.

WORLD WAR I MILITARY PARADE SOUTH ON RIVER STREET TOWARDS MONUMENT SQUARE.

THE RPI APPROACH AT THE FOOT OF BROADWAY. It was erected in 1924 on the former site of one of the original institute buildings that burned in 1904. The Approach was built by the city under Mayor Elias P. Mann, a graduate of the institute in 1872. On October 3, 1924 it was dedicated by Mrs. Elizabeth Van Rensselaer Frazier, a descendant of the founder of RPI, Stephen Van Rensselaer, the patroon. It has fallen in ruins over the years, but there is a movement to rebuild it.

RUSSELL SAGE COLLEGE INAUGURAL DAY, SEPTEMBER 28, 1916. Russell Sage College continues to instruct women to this day, 82 years later.

A VIEW OF THE RPI APPROACH LOOKING UP BROADWAY (EAST). Notice the train attendant stopping traffic as a train backs up. Trains ran through the city up to the late 1950s, and it was common to have to wait for them to cross major streets like Fourth, Sixth, Broadway, and others.

FUNERAL PROCESSION OF BRIG. GEN. JAMES H. LLOYD IN 1911. This cortege is in front of the courthouse. He was captain of the Tibbits Cadets and captain of the Arba Read Steam Fire Company.

DAVID LLOYD GEORGE'S VISIT TO TROY. A liberal reformer and an early architect of social welfare programs, he was best known as the man who led Great Britain to victory in WW I. This photograph was taken at the Troy Union Station.

FIDO ON THE NORTHEAST CORNER OF BROADWAY AND THIRD NEXT TO THE TIMES BUILDING. The Nathan Warren home is behind the dog and you can barely see the Green building and Cannon Place in the background.

TWO YOUNG LADIES. They are being photographed in front of the Times building on Broadway and Third Street.

TROY'S LAST TEN VETERANS OF THE CIVIL WAR IN 1926.

TROY CITIZEN CORP., 6TH BRIGADE. The brigade was in Buffalo on August 18 through 29, 1892 to quell riots. Originally formed in 1835 and disbanded in 1864, they reformed in 1876 and became part of the National Guard.

ANOTHER PARADE! Troy's firemen are marching south down River Street past the intersection of First Street. The Hall building (now called the Rice building) is on the right.

YOUNG LADY IN SEMINARY PARK. Congress Street and the Rynaldo Apartment House are in the background. The courthouse is on the right and out of view. She may be a student at the nearby Emma Willard School or Russell Sage College.

TIBBITS CADETS FIFE AND DRUM CORPS. Tibbits Cadets was organized in 1877 in honor of Brig. Gen. William B. Tibbits. They became part of the National Guard. They quartered in the old armory that was on Ferry and River Streets.

KIDS AT THE DAY HOME, ON SEVENTH AVENUE, IN 1950. They are working on arts and crafts.

FRANKLIN STOVE WORKS. This iron casket was made for the burial of Ulysses S. Grant, who died in nearby Mt. McGregor on July 23, 1885.

ONE OF THE LAST PARADES DOWN RIVER STREET BETWEEN THE MARKET BLOCK AND FRANKLIN SQUARE. This view is looking south up River Street. A few years after this parade in 1966, urban renewal began tearing down all the buildings in this photograph.

THE FIVE & DIME, C. 1920. F.W. Woolworth's and other stores like H.L. Green's, S.S. Kresge, and W.T. Grants all had soda fountain shops where people could eat and socialize. F.W. Woolworth was at 312 River and later Third Street before urban renewal forced them out.

THE GREEN ISLAND BRIDGE, THIRD ONE AT THIS SITE. It collapsed in 1977 due to a damaged pier support (of the previous bridge). It gave way because of high water due to spring currents. Miraculously, no one was hurt.

Six

RECREATION AND LEISURE

SAILBOATS AND ROWERS ENJOYING THE HUDSON RIVER AT TROY. Steamboats are docked just before the Congress Street Bridge. This rowing team was probably from the Laureate Boat Club, or Troy Yacht Club, or one of many rowing clubs.

THE AMERICAN THEATER ON RIVER STREET. It is advertising talking sound pictures. This theater building still exists.

THE LINCOLN THEATER ON THIRD STREET, C. 1922. Built 1922, it was demolished for a parking lot in 1962.

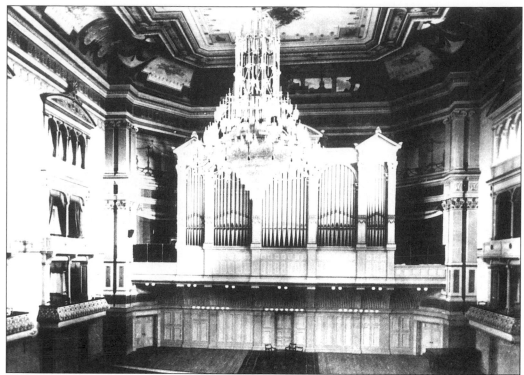

TROY MUSIC HALL, LOCATED IN THE TROY SAVINGS BANK. It has some of the best acoustics in the world. Built in 1875, the Music Hall was dedicated on April 19 by Theodore Thomas with an orchestral and vocal concert. The large organ was placed in 1890. It still hosts concerts today, and recordings are made there because of the great acoustics.

THE TROY THEATER, ON THE WEST SIDE OF RIVER STREET BETWEEN MARKET BLOCK AND FRANKLIN SQUARE. It was torn down during urban renewal. Built in 1922–23, the theater was under the management of Mark Strand Theater Company in New York and Brooklyn. Seats had the Strand name brand on them.

PROCTOR'S THEATER ON THE EAST SIDE OF FOURTH STREET. It was built in 1913–14 as a vaudeville house. Local artist David Lithgow painted the inside murals. Below is an interior view from the stage. It had three levels, two balconies, and side seats. *Parent Trap* was the last movie shown in the early 1970s. The building awaits rebirth.

PROCTOR'S STAGE. Notice the side balconies. A David Lithgow mural graces the top of the stage although you cannot see it in this photograph.

SHEA'S FIVE CENTS THEATER, 18 THIRD STREET, JUST SOUTH OF FREAR'S, C. 1915. Built in 1860, it closed in 1930. Just north of it, adjacent to Frear's, is Griswold Theater. This site had been a theater for more than 60 years when this photograph was taken. The Troy Adelphi was built in 1855 but burned in 1862. Griswold Hall was built in 1871 opening with *The Lady of Lyons*. In 1905 the theater was leased to F.F. Proctor, who remodeled it into a vaudeville house and later a movie theater.

BARKER PARK, C. 1945, THE SITE OF OLD CITY HALL THAT BURNED IN 1938. During the 1950s the park was nicknamed "Pigeon Park" because of the hundreds of pigeons that lived there. "Jim the Peanut Man" would sell you a bag of peanuts or popcorn to feed them. In 1964, the east half was given to St. Anthony's where a new church was built. This was originally the town burial ground.

SEMINARY PARK, ALSO KNOWN AS RUSSELL SAGE PARK ON CONGRESS, SECOND, AND FIRST STREETS. The oldest park in Troy, it still affords citizens relaxation. The park has been modified slightly but basically remains the way it was when it was created two hundred years ago. This photograph was taken *c.* 1900.

Prospect Park on top of Mount Ida, c. 1910. The former Warren estate was purchased in 1913 for a public park. Here an overlook gave a great view of the Hudson Valley. Fountains (pictured below), roads, and walkways ran throughout. The two existing Warren buildings, used as a museum and casino, are now gone. The park has fallen into disrepair. Frear Park (150 acres) was added in 1917. Beman Park (6.28 acres) was one of the first city parks in 1879. Washington Park, between Second and Third Streets, is one of the few private parks in the country. It was established in 1840. Prospect Park was designed by Garrett Baltimore, first African-American graduate of RPI, and civil engineer for Troy.

PROSPECT PARK, MEMORIAL HALL. The Warren family residences, one designed by noted American architect A.J. Davis, were used as a museum and casino until the 1920s. Today they are gone.

TROY BOY'S CLUB IN 1945 AT STATE STREET AND UNION. The building was donated by George B. Cluett in 1911 to help poor boys become better citizens. The club was created in 1899 and still serves Troy youth—both boys and girls as the Troy Boys' and Girls' Club.

TROY BOYS' CLUB. These kids are contemplating their future at Prospect Park during the 1950s. Summer trips to the park were common.

RENSSELAER PARK. Located in Lansingburgh, many a Trojan enjoyed harness races, roller coasters, and other amusement rides, as well as plain fun during the first part of this century. The park closed after WW I. The Rensselaer County Fair was held here as well. The park was located between 108th and 110th Streets and Fifth Avenue. Part of the park was used for the Rensselaer Park Elementary School.

LAUREATE BOAT CLUB, ORGANIZED IN 1866. The boathouse was at the foot of Laureate Avenue (Glen). The Laureate House was built in 1899. The club produced oarsmen, football, and baseball and tennis teams. Here a theatrical group poses as part of the club's annual follies.

PARADISE LOST. The Paradise was a floating casino in Troy that was destroyed by the 1936 flood.

Seven

DISASTERS

FULTON PUBLIC MARKET. After 63 years of public service, it burned on February 18, 1903 in seven hours and 32 minutes. Troy had three major fires, the first in 1820 (burned 1/9th of the city—90 buildings), 1854 (destroyed two hundred buildings in five hours), and 1862 (destroyed 507 buildings, most of downtown, and remarkably only killed five people).

THE MCCARTHY BUILDING FIRE AT MONUMENT SQUARE. Three times within 25 years the McCarthy building and surrounding properties were destroyed by fire. The last was on November 4, 1903, Election Day.

THE BURNING OF CITY HALL ON OCTOBER 28, 1938. Shortly afterwards the site was turned into Barker Park for public use. The park still exists today.

PUBLIC EVENT. Everyone turned out to watch a fire. Notice the steamer pumping as fast as it can at this unknown location.

THE DISASTROUS BOARDMAN BUILDING (BOSTON STORE) FIRE OF JANUARY 6, 1911 AT THE CORNER OF FULTON AND RIVER STREETS. Woolworth's and other buildings north burned as well. Lt. Edward J. Butler of Truck No. 2 was killed by a falling wall. Frear's and the Frear's Annex can be seen in the distance.

FLOOD OF MARCH 28, 1913. One of the worst floods in Troy's history, rising 28 feet above mean low water level. Franklin Square was flooded for the first time. Looking down Congress Street shows water up to Fifth Avenue.

FLOOD OF 1913 LOOKING DOWN FIRST STREET SOUTH OF FERRY STREET. Boats had to be used to go anywhere. Five rowboats are seen in this picture.

THE FLOOD OF 1936, LOOKING NORTH ON RIVER STREET JUST BELOW CHATHAM SQUARE.
This flood rivaled the 1913 flood.

THE FLOOD OF 1936 LOOKING UP FERRY STREET (FOURTH STREET INTERSECTION). The water reached Fifth Avenue as did the one in 1913. Troy continues to have floods although none have been as bad as the 1913 and 1936 floods. This is due to modern flood control efforts north of the city.

THE BLIZZARD OF 1888. On March 13, the city was blanketed with snow. Over 4 feet of snow fell on the Albany-Troy area. This is Chatham Square looking north up King and River Streets.

BLIZZARD OF 1888. This is a view of the Troy Savings Bank at Second and State.

BLIZZARD OF 1888. Most of the buildings between this area of First Street between State and River were banks during the early 19th century and known as Bankers Row.

BLIZZARD OF 1888 LOOKING SOUTH TOWARDS WASHINGTON SQUARE (MONUMENT SQUARE). Cannon Place can be seen in the background. The Soldiers and Sailors Monument had not been built yet.

MOUNT IDA LANDSLIDES. Several occurred during the 19th century. The first in the summer of 1836 did little damage. On January 1, 1837, a slide destroyed three houses and seven people were crushed on the eastern end of Washington Street. On November 14 and 17, 1840, the western slope slid wiping out one house with no injuries. On Friday, February 17, 1843, a large section slipped covering ten buildings and killing 15 people. A fifth slide, on March 17, 1859, saw a large section plunged into Washington Street and buried St. Peter's College, which was just under construction, as depicted in this engraving. You can see the last slide driving along I-90.

TROY'S WORST DISASTER. It would be the ill conceived "urban-renewal" period of the late 1960s and early 1970s that was responsible for most of the destruction of large chunks of Troy's history. Here the north part of the Market Block to Chatham Square is being torn down. Still today, thousands of people flock to Troy to participate in the summer River Fest, or Fall Victorian Stroll. Several development proposals are in the works to rebuild the downtown and beautiful riverfront. There is no doubt that Troy will rise again.